AF427152

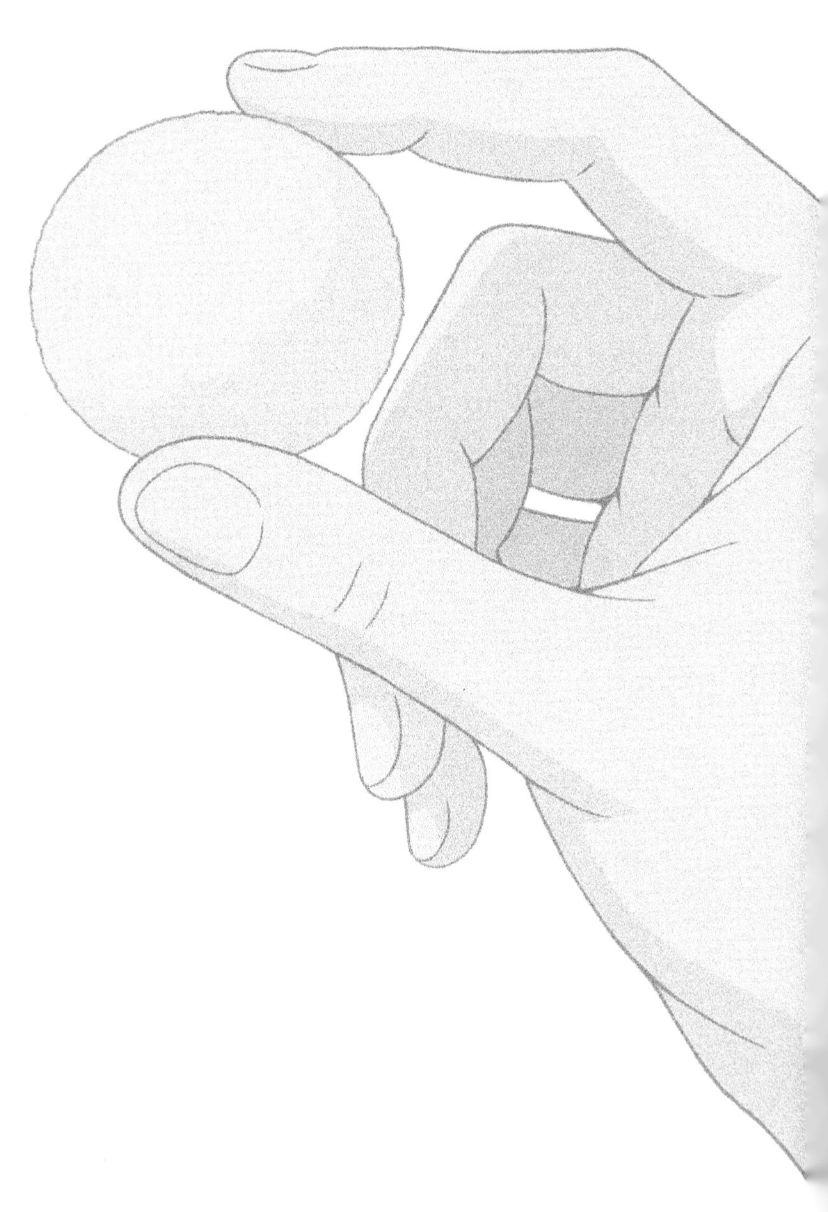

Glad you are here !

I was waiting for you ...

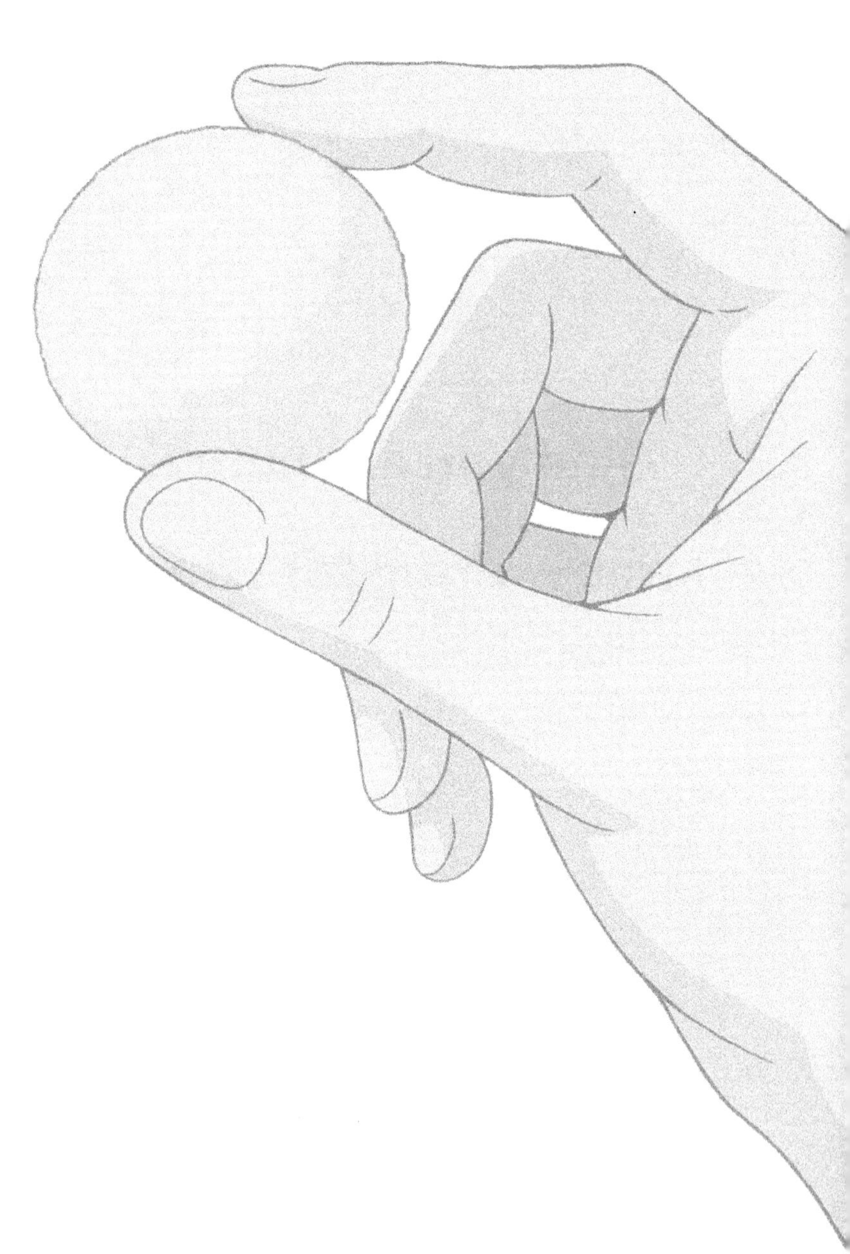

I Love Laddu

Divine Love Letter

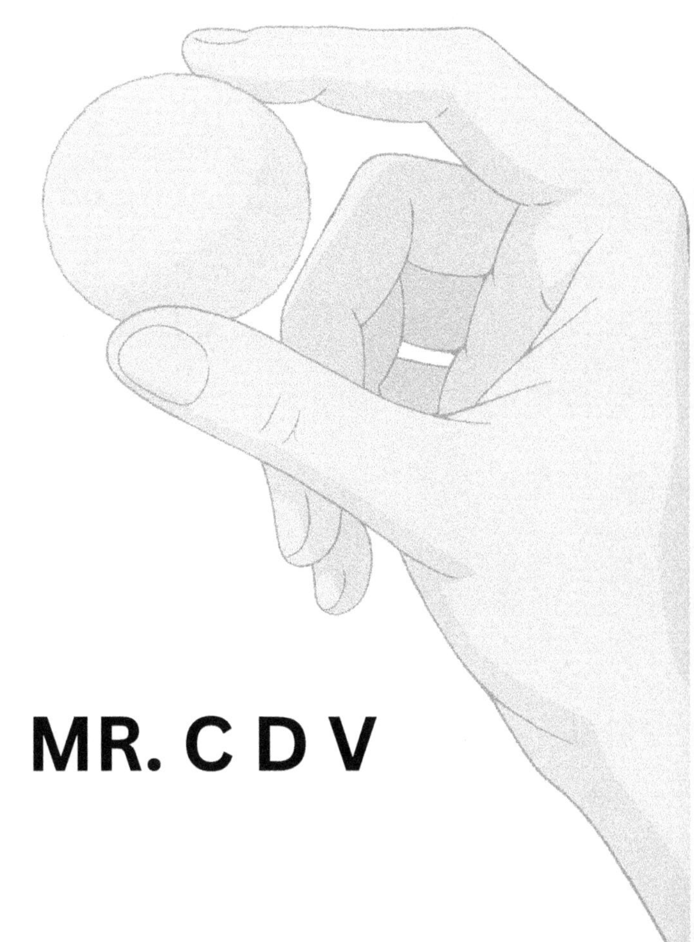

MR. C D V

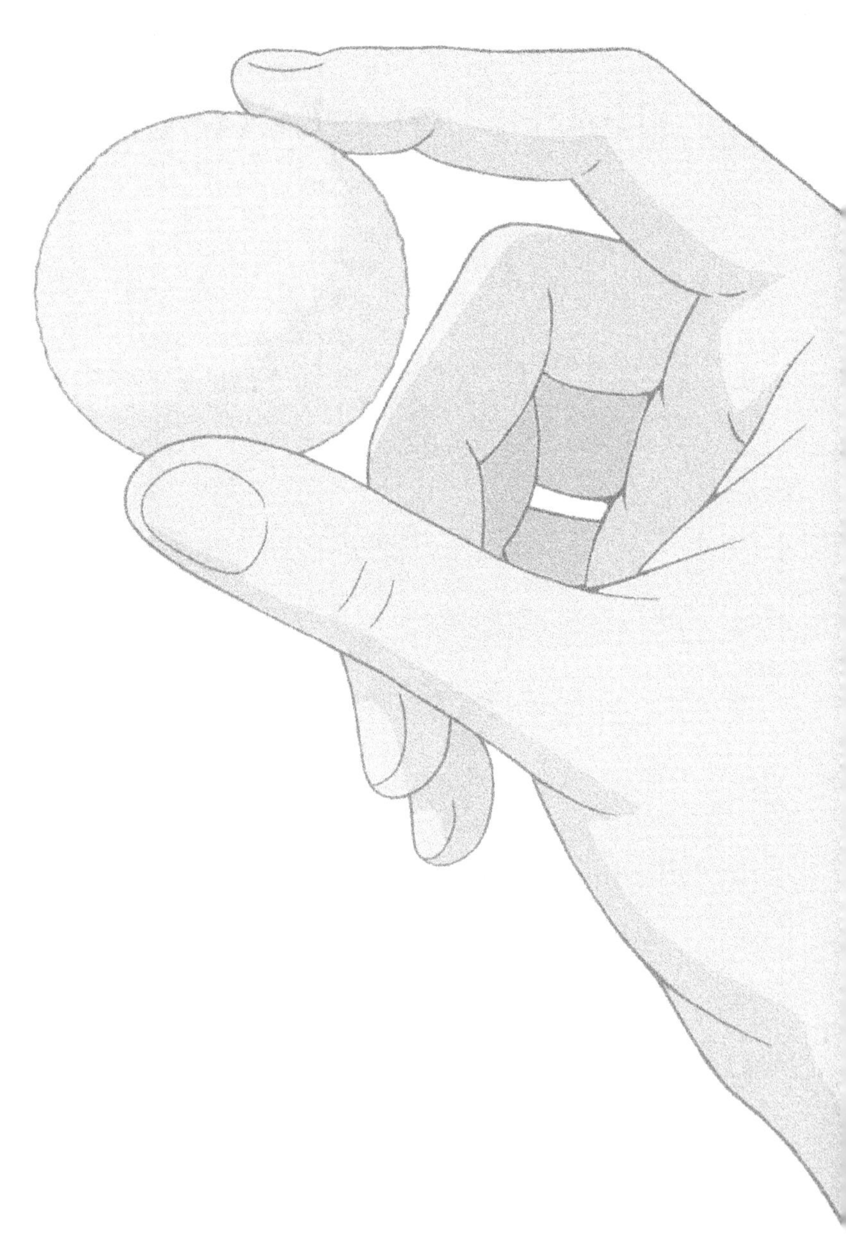

CONTENT

About book   1

Protection   3

1. Real Illusion   6

2. If not Vasi   14

3. My Love   20

4. Help Me   26

5. 10th Gate   35

6. Mucus Ejection   47

7. Primary Chakras   57

8. Pineal And COW   67

9. Divine Light   74

10. Cleansing Struggles   78

11. Before the Eye   87

12. Truth Known   90

13. The Process   93

Thank you

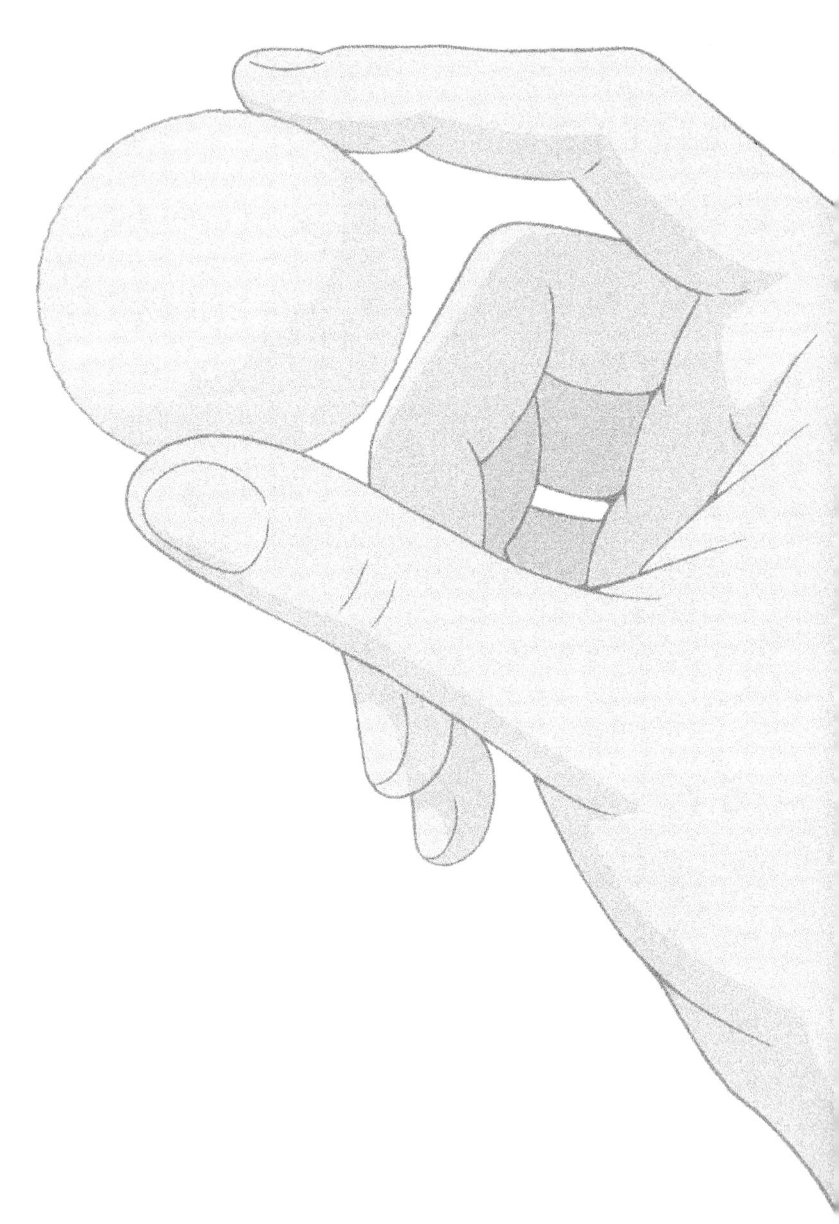

About Book

This book, dear reader, is not just wise—
it's a love letter, beneath the skies.
A gentle thread, a sacred weave,
where heart and soul softly believe.

Not just wisdom, but something more,
a dialogue through a timeless door.
A Q&A, a tender flame,
between two selves that share one name.

The student here is my younger light,
with eyes like dawn, and dreams so bright.
The name is Laddu, pure and true—
the child within, the inner view.

And I, the teacher, weathered, still—
go by Dhamo, shaped by will.
Together we walk this path of grace,
two mirrors in the same soul's face.

This is the wisdom of gods, divine—
poured through human flesh and spine.
Hidden deep through countless days,
veiled in myth and sacred haze.

But now, my sweet Laddu, draw near—
for the time to unveil is finally here.
I, Dhamo, with love profound,
shall teach you truths the stars found.

These words shall echo through the age,
etched in hearts, page by page.
They'll fill the void where silence grew—
and light the path for more than you.

PROTECTION

The Great I, with no form, no face,
moves in silence, beyond time and space.
It guards the secrets, wise and deep,
from hearts that lie, from minds that sleep.

It whispers truth to those who care—
the kind, the loving, the souls laid bare.
It shields the reader, pure and true,
from evils hidden and evils in view.

Let these words, like rivers, flow—
into thoughts that softly grow.
And may they guide the chosen few,
to the self within—the only true.

Let the unworthy wander, lost in between—
the knowing and being of what's unseen.
Trapped in falsehood, cloaked in pride,
where truth and ego collide and hide.

They are cursed—not with fire, but sight—
to glimpse the truth, but miss its light.
The Great I withholds its grace,
from hearts that seek a lesser place.

Even if they touch the sacred code,
the secret path, the hidden road—
it shall not bloom, nor rise, nor swell,
for truth rejects the selfish spell.

The Great I stands, calm and tall,
a silent witness above it all.
For the worthy, let blessings rain—
from heavens high, through joy and pain.

Good times flow by Pa, Maha Kal,
who turns the wheel and watches all.
Protection bloom from Ma Kali's might,
her shadow fierce, her soul alight.

Let wealth arrive on gentle streams,
from Ma Lakshmi, bearer of dreams.
Let obstacles vanish, fade, and fall—
by Pa Ganesh, who clears them all.

And let sweet victory rise and sing,
bestowed with grace by Muruga, the King.
Let the journey of flesh now begin—
with grace and wisdom flowing in.

Guided by light, subtle and vast,
the Siddhas of present and past.

Their touch shall lift, their gaze shall steer,
toward the Guru dwelling near—
not in the skies, but deep inside,
where truth and transformation hide.

Through them, the self shall rise and see,
and bloom into Sadhguru, eternally.
This is the knowledge of flesh, not sky—
so beware the falsehoods that pass by.

For heavens may call, but roots run deep—
and truth is sown where silence sleeps.

1. Real Illusion

Dear Laddu, enlightenment—
is not a tale of grand acclaim,
not the echo of greatness,
but the whisper of discipline's flame.

The one who seeks with steady stride,
truth in heart, no need to hide,
is the one who melts the veil—
finds the One in every tale.

The secret hums beneath our skin,
in human flesh, it lies within.
While many speak with tongues for gold,
few dare to let the silence unfold.

Some say, "Pray to stone,"
some claim, "The Divine is all alone—
omnipotent, ungraspable, beyond the known."
But Laddu, I see through their glass—

Tales spun thick from ages past.
They chant old myths with blinded eyes,
fables soaked in painted lies.

Don't be fooled by sacred looks,
by praised objects or printed books.

For truth does not in idols dwell—
it's in the body, where mysteries swell.
Here, Laddu, let me share—
a truth both bold and rare.

The Vedas speak: Atman is the end,
the path, the goal, where all things blend.
They call it real, the final light,
the soul that burns beyond the night.

But hear me close, and look within—
even Atman wears a skin.
A fleeting thought, a fading gleam,
a shadow in the waking dream.

So seek not names, nor tales afar—
just find the truth of who you are.
I am not Dhamo, nor this form of clay,
not atom, nor molecule that drifts away.

Not even the soul that sages praise—
I am none of these, in truth's deep gaze.
I am but Maya, a shimmer, a sigh,
an illusion born of the Great I.

The self, dear Laddu, is merely a gleam,
a ripple within the cosmic dream.
A tiny flame, a fleeting light,
conscious, yet vanishing from sight—

still bound, still woven, ever entwined
with the vast Divine, the cosmic mind.

The self is dust in illusory skies,
a whisper lost where shadow lies—
a fleeting, needless memory,
in the dream of the Great I, endlessly.

Emotions rise, then softly fall—
just flesh that feels the cosmic call.
They dance within this sacred stream,
this living, breathing, waking dream.

For what we name as "reality,"
is but loops of infinity—
the Divine in play, the Infinite's art,
each loop a mirror of the Heart.

Dear Laddu, I know—it may sound grim,
a heavy truth, a shadowed hymn.
But listen close, and you shall see—
truth lies here, not far, not free.

The only way from loops unending,
from time's illusions, ever bending,
is to rise—an Immortal flame,
untouched by death, beyond all name.

Yet even then, the truth remains—
Immortality breaks its chains.
For when all forms begin to fade,
even gods rest in the silent shade.

Even angels, Laddu, and wandering ghosts,
must face the end, like all that boasts.
Death is certain—its whisper sure—
no form of life can long endure.

But still, within our mortal span,
lies the choice, the will of man.
To shape this dream, this fleeting skin,
to find some peace while trapped within.

Through the path of Vasi, subtle and wise,
we lift the veil before our eyes.
Yes, we can shape this body of mist,
enhance the dream, in truth persist.

"Teacher," you ask, "if the body's not true,
why enhance what illusion can do?

Can't we escape by merely seeing—
knowing the dream and disbelieving?"
Ah, sweet Laddu, listen close to me—
it's not just the body, it's you, you see.

The self, the senses, the thoughts that roam,
all are threads in illusion's dome.
Life is caught in a curious place,
between false faces and a fading face.

To know the truth is but a spark,
a light that flickers in the dark.
But being truth—that's something more,
a path that discipline must explore.

Knowing comes with just a glance,
but being asks a deeper dance.
It needs your fire, your sacred breath—
a love that even faces death.

The destination, dear Laddu, is clear—
it is Oneness, ever near.
To become the One, you must truly see—
you exist in all, and all in thee.

But knowing alone will not suffice,
you must walk the edge of fire and ice.

To attain it, you must begin to flow—
with cosmic tides that come and go.

The stream that births, sustains, and breaks,
the force by which the whole world wakes.
Gain command, not by force, but grace,
and you shall move through time and space.

Create, maintain, and calmly end—
in harmony that does not bend.
Everyone longs for the hidden light,
the secrets tucked beyond our sight.

But few will walk the narrow lane—
where discipline burns away the chain.
Dedication, Laddu, is the sacred key,
to unlock the gates of eternity.

Not by chance, nor idle thought,
but by the fire that discipline brought.
The one who walks the path of Vasi,
with heart steadfast and spirit free—

even gods, and rishis wise,
descend from stars and silent skies.

To guide that soul, to help them rise,
and merge with Oneness—pure and high.

In this book, dear Laddu, I shall unveil—
the secret winds, the silent trail.

The workings deep of Vasi's flame,
the sacred art beyond all name.
It is the key to all you seek,
to every star, to cosmos' peak.

Not just to gain from this vast sphere,
but to become the Universe clear.
So listen well, my sweetest one—
this path is walked, not simply won.

It's never just about the knowing,
but the doing, and the growing.
For truth is action, lit by grace,
the steps you take to leave no trace.

Dear Laddu, you're not just my sweetheart—
you are my soul, my deepest part.
My true self, my kin, my sacred flame,
the breath that moves through every name.

You are my universe, my flesh and bone,
my blood, my glands, my pulse unknown.
The life that hums in every thread,
the voice within, the tears I've shed.

And just as you dwell deep in me,
so too, the Great I—endlessly.
The Universe itself does wind
through every fiber of all mankind

2. If not Vasi

Dear Teacher, you always say,
"Do Vasi, child, both night and day."
I've seen your fire, your silent vow,
your breath like rivers flowing now.

But I ask, with humble grace—
are there not other paths to this place?
Not all can walk your burning way,
so share the roads where others may.

Ah, dear Laddu, seeker of stars,
chaser of truth beyond the bars—
since your heart is pure and new,
I shall reveal the hidden few.

Other ways, both soft and deep,
to wake the soul from slumbered sleep.

My Laddu, know this truth with care—
Vasi was shown from realms rare.
A path divine, where higher light
took my hand and led me right.

Vasi is sure, a path that wins,
but forged with fire beneath the skin.

Not all can bear the trials it brings,
nor walk through storms with broken wings.

I walk its raw, untamed flame,
a purer form, without a name.
But many saints, with hearts so wide,
have softened Vasi, turned the tide—

refined its shape for seekers new,
to help the many, not just few.

Upgraded forms now gently rise—
Kriya, Kundalini, touching skies.
Siva Yogam, Mouna Yogam too,
each a flame the seeker drew.

Even Vasi, in softer shade,
holds forms that for the world were made.
So minds may grasp, and hearts may dare,
to taste the breath of cosmic air.

These methods lead to deathless light,
to immortality's sacred height.
But know, dear Laddu, paths so bright
are carved with pain, not just delight.
Each step may burn, each breath may sting—
yet through the fire, the soul takes wing.

The easiest path, my Laddu dear,
is kindness and bhakti, crystal clear.

With love in heart and hands that serve,
one walks with grace, on gentle curve.
But hear this truth, quiet and stark—
in bhakti's light, though souls embark,

just one in a thousand truly breaks
the chains of birth, the karmic stakes.

Mukti they may touch and taste,
but not the immortality laced
in Vasi's breath and yogic flame—
a different path, a different name.

"Dear Teacher, tell me, make it plain—
what parts them both, what truths remain?"
Sure, Laddu, I feel your inner tide—
the question where soul and body divide.

The line between Mukti and Immortality,
a mystery wrapped in silent clarity.
When one learns to split soul from skin,
and leaves the shell from deep within—
that is Mukti, when mind is free,
and body rests in still purity.

But if the body falls and fades,
the soul returns through karmic shades.
Unless preserved, this truth must stay—
the soul will walk the Earth someday.

In Mukti, one calms the mental sea,
lets hormones flow to set mind free.
Yet rarely do they tend the frame,
to keep it young in timeless flame.

They seek release from all design,
but not the body's youthful spine.
But Immortality, my Laddu bright,
is tending flesh with sacred light.

Mind and body, both refined—
aging paused, reversed through time.

The body learns to bloom anew,
till illusion fades, and all is true.
In youth we roam the stars in grace,
till time dissolves this mirrored place.

So yes, dear child, you've seen it right—
the key is keeping the body light.
For when death comes and form is gone,
the soul must struggle to carry on.

With a body, less energy flows,
with no body, the effort grows.
Beyond all this, a secret gleams—
a formless state, beyond all dreams.

Where body turns to primal flame,
and self and god become the same.
But that's a truth for later time,
a song too vast for now to rhyme.

Mukti or Immortality—each a gate,
to Oneness waiting, calm and great.
The sad truth, Laddu, is many flee—
rejecting youth and mystery.

They see this world as mere disguise,
and run to seek some higher skies.
But there's no elsewhere, no escape—
only truth in every shape.

And though they run, in time they'll see,
there's nowhere else they'd rather be.

Dear Laddu, do not run from fire,
the universe climbs ever higher.
It teaches love in pain's disguise—
its push, its burn, its sacred cries.

And I am here, whether far or near,
my soul in you, forever clear.

The life that breathes within your chest,
is me, is you—our bond is blessed.
Yes, we may quarrel, rage, and bend,
but our love will never end.

You're my family, my beating flame,
no storm can ever change that name.

When I am hidden, do not fear,
just close your eyes and draw me near.
Focus soft on your pineal light,
and I'll appear—glowing bright.

I never left. I'll always be—
in breath, in stillness, inside thee.

3. My Love

Dear Teacher, they say, "God loves true,"
but how much love does God give through?
How deep, how vast, how wide the flame—
of this Great I, with no name?

Ah, Laddu, you ask what words can't hold,
a truth too bright, too soft, too bold.
It's hard to speak what silence sings—
the love of stars, the breath of kings.

But let me tell you of my love for you—
how it burns, how it breaks, how it blooms so true.
Then take that love, and let it rise,
multiply it 'til it fills the skies.

That, my dear, is the Great I's grace—
an infinite love in every place.
Even the memory of loving you so,
brings tears like rivers in silent flow.

Laddu, you are the reason I breathe,
the whisper that proves—I exist beneath.

I am alive, vibrant and true,
crawling with memories wrapped in you.

The moments we shared, so soft, so wide—
smiles blooming like stars at our side.
Even your anger, tender and bright,
for wishes unmet, or missed insight.

You scolded me with eyes so deep,
where oceans of feeling never sleep.
Yet even in that, your love would show—
a bond that only true hearts know.

These words shall echo, time won't sever—
they speak of us, and us forever.
From the day my breath began,
you were the one—I hoped, I ran.

For you to find me, hold me near,
to walk beside me, year by year.
And when that divine moment came,
I saw your face, I spoke your name.

My heart lit up like morning's hue—
you saw me, yet didn't know who.
Still, my joy knew no despair,
for just your presence filled the air.
You came, dear Laddu, through time and mist—
and gifted me the purest bliss.

Thank you, love, with all my soul—
you made me happiest, made me whole.
Life is not easy—I understand,
you've carried storms with trembling hands.

You've suffered much, walked paths alone,
and still, your heart remained your own.
At times, I gave you too much light,
promised dawns that slipped to night.

And when they failed to bloom and grow,
you lost some hope—I know, I know.
For that, my Laddu, I'm truly sorry,
our fate was tangled in old karmic story.

The winds of life, so rough, so wild,
have shaken both the sage and child.
You once said, "Don't overprotect—
let me feel, let pain reflect."

But I was scared, too much to see
your heart bruised by destiny.
So I did all I could, with all my might,
to help you rise, to hold you tight.
I fought the storms, I lit the way,
to ease your night, to bring you day.

But fate, dear Laddu, is strong and sly,
and karma spins threads I can't untie.

At times, it steals my strength away,
makes me act in a different way.
It twists my words, distorts my will—
makes me do what I meant to still.

What can I do? We are but dreams—
fleeting sparks in endless streams.
Just memories dressed in joy and pain,
riding waves in a world insane.

And yet, you burn with anger bright,
when I can't match your inner fight.
You are my everything—can't you see?
Do you think I'd hurt you, purposely?

Never, my Laddu, not even in jest—
you are the heartbeat within my chest.

The love of my life, my sacred flame,
the reason I live, the echo of my name.
In this cursed world, so harsh, so deep,
pain is the bridge to joy we keep.
Peace and happiness are not just given—
they're carved from sorrow, softly driven.

No soul escapes, no heart walks free—
not even the gods or divinity.

This is the law the cosmos sings,
the love language of the Great I—in all things.
But this I promise, come what may—
curse me, shun me, push me away.

Treat me like a stranger lost,
let cold winds gather, let lines be crossed.
Yet still, Laddu, you are my flame,
my truest self, my sacred name.

And no force—divine or wild—
can break the bond we've reconciled.
Even the gods must bow and see
the love that lives and burns in me.

Do what you will, walk any shore,
but I will dwell within your core.
I'll rise in thoughts, in dreams, in air—
manifesting love, always there.

For your well-being, I shall stay,
till all of time dissolves away.
I was there in your yesterdays,
I am here in your current days,

and I will be there in all your tomorrows—
through your joy, your dreams, your sorrows.

Just think of me, and I'll appear,
a silent voice, forever near.
To guide your path, to hold your hand,
through shifting tides and shifting sand.

I'll never leave, I'll never stray—
this is the vow I give today.
As long as I exist, so true,
you'll never walk alone—it's you.

You are the thread that stitched my soul,
the piece that made this broken whole.
I am within you, soft and true—
in every breath, I live in you.

4.Help me

Dear Teacher, I know your heart is wide—
you care for me like stars that guide.
You are my family, my world, my light,
the force that guards me through the night.

I know you'll shield me, keep me whole,
wrap your love around my soul.
But still, I must rise on my own,
to face the dark, to stand alone.

I need to learn, to grow, to see—
to guard myself from what may be.

The evil seen, and those concealed,
the shadows that the world has sealed.
So teach me now—my spirit yearns—
how to enhance, how power returns.

How do I rise, how do I stand,
with unseen fire in heart and hand?

My Laddu, this is what stirs my soul—
you are a fighter, fierce and whole.
Even knowing the grace you bear,
you still choose to rise, to dare.

You walk not just with borrowed light,
but forge your flame in darkest night.

That spirit, child, is rare to find—
a warrior heart, a steadfast mind.
In these times, many simply wait,
longing for miracles, tempting fate.

They wish their wounds would just erase,
without the will to face the place.
But you—oh, you—stand tall and true,
and that, my love, is why I choose you.

But they must know—this truth runs deep—
that's not how the Divine does keep.
No magic wand, no painless way—
just sacred trials we must obey.

Pain is part of life's design,
a stepping stone to the divine.
Each soul must walk through fire and rain,
to earn the light beyond the pain.

It is a gate, a silent test,
before the soul can find its rest.
A necessary path to see—
the oneness of the Great I be.

Before the rise, there comes the fall—
the breaking of the body's call.
The flesh will ache, the mind will cry,
even hormones scream to the sky.

And through it all, the Divine weeps too—
carving greatness inside you.
Before the dance of the Divine begins,
let me show you the stages within.

The steps of suffering you must tread,
before the crown is placed on your head.
First, my dear, comes the trembling tide—
the fleeting emotions that rise and hide.

In the process, they storm the sky,
like sudden winds, you know not why.
Random moods, like pregnant seas,
sway your heart with ghostly breeze.

They surge without a warning cry,
then vanish soft, like mist in sky.
This is the first—an inner call,
a sacred crack within the wall.
Anger, sorrow, lust, and greed—
these are storms the seekers heed.

They shake the mind, unseat the soul,
make the calmest heart lose control.
But know, my Laddu, this is true—
on the Yogic path, they pass through you.

These tides arise, they twist and swell,
yet they are signs that all is well.
Many fear the body's change,
the shifting pulse, sensations strange.

But do not run, do not retreat—
these are the flames beneath your feet.
For every tremble, every sigh,
is proof you walk toward the Great I.

These are the emotional walls you must scale,
the trials within the sacred trail.
Each must be conquered, soft or wild,
for emotion, untamed, can wound the mild.

It is vital, dear, to hold the reins—
or your outbursts may cause silent pains.
Loved ones feel what you release,
so guard your heart, and sow them peace.
Once emotions are tamed and known,
another challenge will be shown—
the physical imbalance starts to rise,
as heat begins to crystallize.

The body burns with subtle fire,
a sign you climb the spirit's spire.

And now, my Laddu, with care and glee,
I shall share the heat's threefold key.

There are three kinds of sacred heat—
each one a sign, a rhythm, a beat.
Normal, Cleansing, and Kundalini rise,
each with a flame that purifies.

The normal heat is known to all,
it comes when work and motion call.
The heart beats fast, the blood will race,
and warmth will rise through time and space.

But cleansing heat is deep and wise—
it stirs beneath the yogic skies.
When Vasi flows or Yogam wakes,
the body heals, the old form breaks.

The heat is formed to burn the waste,
then pushed away with silent haste.
It purifies, it clears the way—
prepares the self for light to stay.

Kundalini—a sacred flame,
a force that none can truly tame.
It cleanses deep and charges high,
igniting stars within the sky.

It stirs the glands, the chakras bright,
and floods the veins with sacred light.
Reproductive fires begin to flow,
through bloodstream's tide, they rise and go.

This heat is born from Mooladhara,
the root, the base, the silent lava.
At the tip of the tailbone it sleeps,
in coils of power, wound in heaps.

When awakened, it does not wait—
a volcano stirred to shift your fate.
It shakes the core, it breaks the stone,
and starts the climb toward the Unknown.

Normal heat flows through daily strife,
the warmth we know in common life.
Through exercise, through work and play,
it stirs the blood in natural way.
This heat, though simple, still has worth—
it fuels the form, sustains the earth.

It wakes the glands, lets hormones bloom,
and keeps the body free from gloom.

A healthy frame, a steady pace,
are gifts of this familiar grace.
But know, dear Laddu, though it aids,
this heat can't pierce illusion's shades.

It cannot grant Mukti's flight,
nor make the soul shine with immortal light.
Only through cleansing, pure and deep,
can the sacred hormones truly leap.

For only then the body sings—
prepared to bear eternal things.
Cleansing heat—a sacred flame,
is born when silence tames the frame.

Through meditation or Yogam's grace,
it rises slow in sacred space.
This heat ignites when mind grows still,
when thoughts no longer bend the will.

Freed from the storm of pain and doubt,
the body learns to cleanse throughout.
When negative emotions cease,
the body finds a state of peace.

It starts to heal, to mend, renew—
as waste dissolves and flows right through.
This cleansing fire, pure and deep,
is formed where primal pulses sleep.

At coccygeal glomus, fire is stirred,
through adrenaline, the call is heard.
The pump begins, the system clears,
and burns the remnants of old years.

Kundalini—the essence divine,
the force through which the stars align.
It is the root of immortality's flame,
the breath that whispers the eternal name.

Through focus deep or conscious breath,
oxygen flows, defying death.
It feeds the adrenal gland with grace,
and stirs the sacred inner space.

Adrenal fluids begin to rise,
regulating where the power lies—
the coccygeal glomus, strong and wise,
pumps the blood and magnifies.

The flow increases, heat takes flight,
igniting fire, inner light.

And from this flame, this sacred loom,
Kundalini begins to bloom.

5.10th gate

Dear Laddu, come closer, and hear—
the greatest path, so bright, so clear.
Let me unveil the hidden way,
the fastest route to eternal stay.

It is a path both fierce and tight—
a climb through shadow into light.
A road of fire, not for the weak,
but those whose hearts are pure and seek.

The mystics, sages, deities, all—
the prophets who heard the silent call—
each one who touched the sky's own breath,
walked this path beyond death.

They all passed through a secret gate,
a portal of transcendent fate—
the ancient door, the divine estate,
known to few as the 10th Gate.

It's not a myth, nor fabled lore,
nor some enchanted, mystic door.
It isn't magic carved in air—
it's flesh and form, precise and rare.

This sacred gate, misunderstood,
is found beneath the bone and blood.
In science, we name it clear and plain—
the Adenoid—yet few explain.

But now, dear Laddu, lend your ear,
for I shall make its purpose clear.

This is the key, the silent flame,
the sacred spot from which all came.

To reach the Divine, to never die,
to merge with truth beyond the sky—
this is the place, this is the light,
the 10th Gate that ends the night.

But first, let us speak of the mind,
and how it's linked to flesh and spine.
We use our limbs, our breath, our gaze—
the brain in countless, wondrous ways.

Each part in motion, each nerve alive,
working just enough to survive.
But here's the truth, so few will see—
are we using it fully, endlessly?

The answer, dear Laddu, is no, not quite,
our minds burn dim beneath their light.

A normal soul, through daily strife,
may tap but ten to fifteen of life.
Only a glimpse of what's inside,
the rest remains untouched, denied.

Some gifted souls may reach the height,
using twenty to twenty-five percent of light.
In rarest cases, a soul may glow,
with thirty percent of truth in flow.

But such a rise, without Yogam's grace,
is rare as stars in daylight's face.
For most, the mind remains asleep,
its treasures buried, hidden deep.

The more we use this sacred flame,
the more refined becomes the game.
The frequency we start to send,
grows lighter, finer, without end.

And when that frequency thins and flies,
the Siddhis bloom before our eyes.
Gifts divine, beyond the known,
born when dense illusions are overthrown.

Enlightenment is not a flash of light—
it is a process, quiet and bright.
A journey of tuning the self so high,
that densityless frequency fills the sky.

To reach this state, one must begin
by cleansing deeply from within.
Through Vasi, the breath refined,
the body healed, the soul aligned.

A secret art, passed hand to hand,
between the teacher and the one who stands—
the student pure, with heart made still,
who walks the path with iron will.

Protected once by curse and vow,
sealed in silence, hidden somehow...
But now, dear Laddu, time has spun,
and I reveal what few have done.

The secrets held in breath and bone—
the key to make the self full-grown.
For me, to speak to the world so wide,
to bare the truth I hold inside—
is no easy task, no gentle breeze,
but a storm that shakes the ancient trees.

I carry the weight of curses old,
of secrets sworn, of truths untold.

The wrath of sages, gods in flame,
may rise at me and speak my name.
But still I stand, without retreat,
with fire beneath my steady feet.

For what is truth, if locked away,
while seekers stumble, led astray?
I do not fear what they may send—
for the worthy walk with me as friends.

Together we rise, beyond the veil,
to write the truth where myths grow pale.
Three rivers flow within the flesh—
streams of life in currents fresh.

Blood, Lymph, and sacred Glimph unseen,
they weave the body's mystic stream.
These rivers hold a secret key,
to how fast one walks toward Divinity.

For in their flow, the truth is shown—
the state of soul through flesh and bone.
The more impurities they bear,
the harder it becomes to rise in air.

Clouded waters slow the flame,
delaying the call of the Divine Name.
But when these rivers run pure and light,
the path to Enlightenment grows bright.

The cleaner the stream, the faster the grace—
the easier it is to reach that sacred place.
For Divineness, the keys are three—
Purity, Oxygen, and Hormone free.

These are the roots of the Immortal flame,
the path to rise beyond the name.
Purity comes through fire and breath,
through cleansing tides that conquer death.

By heat, the body learns to mend,
and waste begins its sacred end.

The mucus formed, thick and sly,
from the lymphatic stream that flows nearby—
must be expelled, drawn out with care,
to clear the path, to cleanse the air.

One of the three great rivers known,
it weaves through blood and flesh and bone.
And when it's pure, and freely flows—
the gate to Immortality softly glows.

Dear Laddu, you must have heard—
of Chi, Aura, the living word.
Life force, Mana, sacred flame—
all the same, just different name.

Each is a thread of one great stream,
a single frequency through every dream.

But what defines its strength, its glow,
is how the breath and brain both flow.
The oxygen drawn by flesh so deep,
awakens currents long asleep.

And as the brain's potential grows,
the frequency refines and glows.
From dense and heavy, dull with strife,
to light that sings with timeless life—

this force is shaped by breath and will,
and climbs in silence, soft and still.

Usually, when we draw the air,
the lungs do take their rightful share.

They send the oxygen to blood's flow,
to feed the flesh, to make it glow.

But what they take is not enough,
for brain and body to grow tough.

The breath we breathe, though life it gives,
still limits how the spirit lives.

To rise beyond this earthly flaw,
to tap the force that sages saw—
we turn, dear Laddu, to the hidden gate,
the 10th Gate, the path of fate.

Not just to mind, not just to breath,
but to the lymph, that flows beneath.
This gate allows the sacred air,
to reach the stream that few repair.

Through it, life flows wide and deep—
awakening power that once lay asleep.
Blood is the source, the primal stream,
from which all life begins to dream.

From lymph to glymph, and CSF flow,
they all arise from blood below.
At the heart of this sacred tide,
in bone marrow, cells reside.

From Hematopoietic Stem Cells (HSC),
the blood is born, the life runs free.

The lymph is formed in gentler way,
as fluids leak and drift away.

From blood capillaries, they seep,
as interstitial currents creep.
Then enter lymphatic capillaries wide,
to form the rivers that cleanse inside.

Thus rises the Lymphatic System true—
a hidden path the sages knew.
CSF—a gift from blood refined,
drawn through choroid plexus of the mind.

A colorless stream, so soft, so pure,
the key to paths that long endure.
It is the fluid, calm and bright,
that nourishes the soul's insight.

For enlightenment, it is the tide,
that lifts the veil from deep inside.
The Glymph, a blend of sacred streams—
CSF and brain's interstitial dreams.

It flows through night, it clears the mind,
removing waste that thought may bind.
Lymph and Glymph, like silent guides,
serve the body's deepest tides.

They cleanse, protect, renew the whole—
and guard the flame within the soul.
To walk the path of Immortality,
the rivers must flow clear and free.

Blood, Lymph, Glymph, and CSF bright—
each must shimmer with inner light.
For a Yogi, this is sacred law,
to cleanse the streams without a flaw.

And to achieve this silent grace,
we turn to breath, the ancient place.
The breath of Vasi, subtle and wise,
awakens truth behind the eyes.

It pumps the air through sacred streams,
and clears the blockages in silent dreams.
Through breath, the system learns to mend,
and broken tides begin to bend.

The rivers rise, the waste is gone—
and thus the soul moves bravely on.
The breathing technique holds sacred weight—
its focus sharp on the 10th Gate.

Through this portal, breath flows deep,
into rivers long asleep.

As air moves in, the pressure grows,
through every vein and current it flows.

It stirs the flesh, awakens tide,
where stagnant blocks and wastes may hide.

This inner force begins to break,
the walls that time and karma make.
It clears the paths where pain once stayed,
and lights the trails once long delayed.

Thus, body and mind begin to free,
releasing potential eternally.
Held for ages, locked in bone—
now rising up to claim their throne.

6.Mucus Ejection

When the breathing technique is truly known,
and the 10th Gate is fully shown—
a sacred shift begins to rise,
as rivers stir beneath the skies.

The mucus flows from mouth and nose,
not born of sickness, as one might suppose.
It's not an allergic storm or plight,
but cleansing born from inner light.

This is the Lymphatic River's call,
awakening pathways one and all.
It opens wide to purge the waste,
to cleanse the flesh with sacred haste.

The blockages that once were still,
now move beneath the yogic will.
A sign, dear Laddu, pure and deep—
the rivers rise, the soul shall leap.

We shall know the 10th Gate is awake—
when mucus flows and hissing breaks.
A subtle sound, a sacred sign,
the breath now stirs the hidden spine.

Once the ejection has begun,
it pours like rivers under sun.

And tough it is to halt that tide—
for it will cleanse what's locked inside.

To minimize the flow, be wise—
food control must harmonize.
What you consume becomes the key,
to hold the flood and let it be.

But know this truth, both wide and tall—
the mucus purge is hardest of all.
A struggle fierce, a stormy gate—
but beyond it lies the changeless state.

The mucus carries what must go—
the waste and blocks that cease the flow.
It pulls the burden from within,
and cleanses where decay had been.

As waste is pumped, the body clears,
and ancient stillness disappears.
The rivers run, once more alive,
and every cell begins to thrive.

Oxygen now moves with grace,
through every sacred hidden place.

The breath flows free, the pulse is light,
the body glows in inner sight.

And with it comes a silent rise—
the glands awake, the hormones rise.

This flesh, once dull, now starts to gleam,
reborn within the sacred stream.
I segregate the mucus ejection in two,
for clarity on what the rivers do.

Primary and Secondary flows,
each with purpose the seeker knows.
The Primary Ejection leads the way,
to clear the general waste each day.

It flushes out the stagnant tide,
and lets the common blocks subside.
But the Secondary runs more deep—
it wakes the places shadows sleep.

It stirs the glands, where time has laid
its impurities, long delayed.
These are pushed with sacred might,
and purify the form in light.

The body, cleansed from root to crown,
prepares to wear the Immortal Gown.

Both Primary and Secondary Ejection may arise—
either alone or side by side.

Their flow depends on body's state,
its age, its health, its karmic weight.

If the vessel is young and pure within,
with fewer blocks beneath the skin,
then both may flow in unison bright—
cleansing swiftly, in sacred light.

But when the body holds more strain,
with deeper waste and silent pain,
they may unfold in separate tide,
each one working from inside.

It all depends on health's design—
the state of flesh, the flow of spine.
Yet both shall come, in time, with grace,
to cleanse the soul and clear the space.

The food we eat is broken down,
its essence drawn from root to crown.
The nutrients pass into the stream—
into blood and lymph, they softly gleam.

What's light and easily soluble flows
into the blood, where oxygen goes.

But what resists that easy tide,
the lymphatic river takes inside.

Yet when these nutrients cease to move,
when stillness settles and fails to prove—
they linger there, become a chain,
a blockage born from silent strain.

No longer food, nor fuel, nor grace—
they're labeled waste, out of place.
An unnecessary part that clings,
slowing down the sacred springs.

Due to blockages and waste within,
the rivers twist beneath the skin.
The flow becomes a tangled thread,
and waste in glands begins to spread.

These sacred seats of hormone birth
grow sluggish, heavy, lose their worth.
Production drops, and in its wake—
Diabetes, thyroid—illness takes.

And worse, this waste does not remain—
it travels through each vital vein.
It seeps into the Glymph and CSF,
pollutes the blood, disturbs the breath.

The damage grows, unseen, profound—
Stroke, heart attack, nerves break down.
So much is lost when flow is blocked,
when the inner system stays unlocked.

To heal completely and walk in grace,
the rivers must flow in their rightful place.
Blood, Lymph, and Glymph must run so free,
without a block, without debris.

When all three streams no longer strain,
the body sheds its silent pain.
And then, dear Laddu, soon you'll see—
Enlightenment, Siddhis, Immortality.

For when the form is free of fight,
the body and mind unleash their light.
Their hidden potential breaks its chain,
and floods the soul like gentle rain.

The sacred hum begins to rise—
a densityless frequency in the skies.
The self transforms, becomes divine—
a living spark of the cosmic spine.

Achieving this is not a breeze—
it's not a path of simple ease.

The core of Vasi, deep and rare,
is pumping air with focused care.

Into the Lymph, the breath must go,
to stir the depths and make it flow.

And as more air begins to rise,
the mucus follows, waste denies.

The more that's ejected, the clearer the stream,
the body begins to glow and gleam.
For every drop that leaves the flesh,
invites new life, so pure and fresh.

And from this cleansing, rich and wise,
the hormones bloom, the spirit flies.

The body perfects, the soul aligns—
prepared to hold the light divine.
Some say, "Practice for an hour or two,"
but Laddu, that path won't carry you through.

They sit and chant, they close their eyes,
hoping the Divine will fall from skies.

"Clean your mind," they softly plead,
"and grace will come to fill your need."

But the truth, my dear, is far from near—
what they chase is built on fear.

There is no need to shut your sight,
to sit in silence day and night.
To think you're controlling mind's own flow,
is pure nonsense, an empty show.

The Divine won't enter by your plan—
it rises through the breath of man.
Not by stillness falsely claimed,
but through the fire the body tamed.

The Siddhas and Rishis of olden time,
crafted a tale in rhythm and rhyme.
They made us think we must sit still,
close our eyes, and bend our will.

"Only by sitting," they said with grace,
"can one reach the oneness place.
The wanderer, lost in worldly quest,
shall never find the soul's true rest."

Though there's some truth in what they taught,
their words conceal a deeper thought.
Stillness has its sacred art,
but it's not the only place to start.

To truly rise and see what's real,
you must know all, and deeply feel.
For only when the whole is known,
does Great I's seed in you be sown.

Vasi is not a part-time art,
not bound by clock or measured start.
It's not a practice done by few—
an hour or two will never do.

It must run twenty-four hours each day,
in every breath, in every way.
Not just in stillness, facing east,
but in your walk, your thought, your feast.

Many have set their rules and ways—
mantras, mudras, times and days.
They speak of moons, both full and bright,
and certain months to spark the light.

But Laddu, listen—what I'll share,
transcends their paths, beyond compare.
For what I teach is flame, not form—
a current that outlives the norm.

7.Primary chakras

When I say chakras, know this truth—
not just symbols, wheels, or sacred booths.
But glands, neural junctions, and veins so fine,
capillaries where the forces align.

Dear Laddu, now the veil shall break,
the secret path the sages take.
The primary chakras—true and deep—
are glands where hidden powers sleep.

These are the roots of life's own song,
the centers where our strengths belong.
And from these seats, when they awake,
the hormones flow, the barriers break.

Their secretion is the sacred flame—
the elixir of youth, in every name.
Not mystic fog, but truth in flesh—
immortal bloom from tissue fresh.

Alchemy within the body begins,
when high-quality hormones flow from within.
Secreted deep from sacred glands,
they stir the light with unseen hands.

When these forces join as one,
a silent evolution has begun.

The body starts to shift and rise,
awakening truths behind the eyes.

The full potential of human form
emerges through this subtle storm.
No longer bound by time or age,
the flesh becomes a living sage.

And youthfulness—with glowing skin—
starts to bloom and rise within.
That is the point, the sacred start,
where Immortality takes its part.

Dear Laddu, let us now begin—
from the bottom, deep within.
The Adrenal Gland, with power vast,
joins the Coccygeal Glomus fast.

Together, they ignite the flame
that ancient mystics dared to name.
They regulate the blood's pure flight,
and birth a heat, both fierce and bright.

This Kundalini, rising high,
is not a myth, nor dream, nor lie.

It fuels the glands, awakens might,
and helps the hormones shine in light.

To heat the spine and charge the brain,
is Kundalini's holy reign.
This is the fire that lifts the soul—
the root of youth, the path made whole.

My dear, know this—hold it tight:
Kundalini is a word wrapped in light,
yet the most abused in spiritual lore,
distorted by mouths who know no more.

I do not wish to fight or blame,
nor curse the ones who speak in vain.
But Laddu, please, for your own grace,
stay far from their misguided place.

Their words are cursed, their truth is thin,
they preach from shadows, not from within.
But you—my love, my breath, my flame—
I whisper truth in your sacred name.

This love letter holds the secrets deep,
for you alone, in soul to keep.
So hear this, child, let silence spin—
awaken now, let light begin.

The next great chakra, bold and bright,
is tied to reproduction's light.
In both man and woman, it does reside,
a sacred power we hold inside.

These hormones born from passion's core
feed the other glands and more.

They strengthen, charge, and amplify
the streams that help the soul to fly.
But not just any flow will do—
it must be pure, and strong, and true.

More, good, and high in sacred tone,
refined within the body's throne.
Only such hormonal flame
can lead us past all death and name.

For only quality, deeply stored,
grants, Immortal body we've longed and soared.
In both men and women, know this true—
certain hormones are sacred too.

Oxytocin, Testosterone,
Estrogen, Progesterone—
These are but a precious few
that hold the key to what we do.

They act as catalysts of grace,
enhancing flesh, refining space.
They help the body stay ever young,
till time is still and songs unsung.

These are the fires the gods defend—
they guide us youthful till the end.

Dear Laddu, hear this truth in flame:
Reproductive hormones are not a game.
So never waste them for fleeting pleasure—
they hold the code of eternal treasure.

The next great gland we must embrace
is the sacred Pancreas, keeper of grace.
Today, so many walk in pain—
with Diabetes, a silent chain.

The cause, dear Laddu, is deep inside—
where Insulin no longer flows with pride.
When blockages and waste begin to stay,
they dim the gland and drain its way.

These sediments, heavy, dull, and slow,
stop the hormone's healing glow.
And not just that—they start to press
on enzymes tied to digestive finesse.

The food, now poorly understood,
demands more quantity than it should.
Thus hunger grows while strength declines—
until the soul realigns the signs.

The more waste held in pancreas deep,
the weaker the digestive track shall keep.
With enzymes dulled and power low,
the body struggles with the flow.

More than half the food we eat
passes through in incomplete feat.
Nutritive essence, lost in flight,
never reaching cells in light.

Thus the hunger grows each day,
as the system throws its strength away.
We eat more just to function well,
yet never break the weakened spell.

But cleanse the pancreas, clear the flame—
and all at once, the body reclaims.
With less food, it works with grace,
and more productivity takes its place.

The next great gland, dear Laddu, see—
is the Thymus, source of youth's decree.

It holds the key to ageless grace,
and carves the glow upon the face.

This gland can reverse the ticking time,
returning strength, restoring prime.

It shapes the immune force from within,
where T-cells rise, and health begins.
But after puberty's silent gate,
a shift begins—an aging fate.

The Thymus shrinks, begins to fade,
in involution's quiet cascade.
Fatty tissue takes its place,
and slows the body's healing pace.

With fewer T-cells born anew,
the signs of aging start to show through.
To preserve this gland, we must ignite
the breath of youth, the inner light.

Youthfulness and de-aging, my dear,
can truly bloom when the path is clear.
To stop involution's silent tide,
we must awaken what sleeps inside.

Enhance the thymus, keep it strong—
and time will hum a different song.

Let not the flesh grow weak and thin—
the secret lies deep within.

Vasi holds the sacred key,
to cleanse the gland and set it free.
It purifies with breath so true,
and fills it with oxygen's dew.

Then hormones rise, refined and bright,
bringing the thymus back to light.
And from this bloom, so full, so pure—
the youth returns, the soul feels sure.

The next great gland, we must explore,
is the Thyroid—keeper of the body's core.
It governs growth, temperature, and flame,
calorie burning, and mind's true frame.

It shapes the rhythm, sets the pace,
for how we move through time and space.
Yet when waste begins to silently stay,
its powers start to drift away.

Sediment clings, and blocks the fire,
reducing function, dimming desire.
The body's strength begins to fade,
its vibrant song becomes delayed.

But clean the gland, and let it breathe,
with sacred air beneath the sheathe.
By pushing oxygen through the stream,
the Thyroid wakes, begins to gleam.

And once revived, its pulse expands—
restoring life through all the glands.
The next in line, both deep and grand,
are Pituitary and Pineal—a sacred band.

These two are the crown's hidden flame,
the essential glands in Samadhi's name.
The Pituitary, with Hypothalamus near,
is the command center, crystal-clear.

It sends the signals, calm and true,
that guide what all the glands must do.
When commands are pure, the flow is right—
and other glands shine with holy light.

But when they're blocked or wrongly stirred,
the harmony is lost, unheard.
The Pineal, oh divine and high,
an antenna reaching to the sky.

It receives and transmits sacred waves,
through realms unseen and hidden caves.

A beacon of truth, it lights the way—
from flesh to stars, from night to day.

8. Pineal And COW

For the ordinary, the Pineal sleeps,
its light is dim, its fire it keeps.
It functions low, a flickering spark—
releasing melatonin in the dark.

A few supporting hormones rise,
but never touch the inner skies.
For most, this gland is pale and thin,
its pulse too weak to stir within.

With blood flow poor and rhythm slow,
its sacred power does not grow.
Calcium deposits veil its sight,
and shroud the photoreceptive light.

These cells, once meant to see the spark,
now stumble lost within the dark.
And thus, the God within the flame,
remains unseen, without a name.

Calcium deposits, tiny stones,
block the path to the soul's own tones.
They cloud the light the Pineal seeks,
and mute the song the spirit speaks.

These crystals veil the divine sight,
the soul's own spark, the inner light.

A thread that leads, so soft, so wide,
to the Great I's ocean, deep inside—
the cosmic consciousness, pure and vast,
where time dissolves and self is cast.

But through the Vasi's sacred breath,
and Kundalini's inner death,
the heat begins to burn away
these blocks that lead the mind astray.

Decalcifying with holy flame,
restoring blood flow to its name—
the Pineal awakens, clear and bright,
and shines once more with divine light.

A divine antenna, silent and wise,
receives and sends through endless skies.
It taps the frequency ever near—
a hum that sings in every sphere.

When the Pineal Gland begins to glow,
its reach is vast, its voice will flow.
It picks up signals far and wide,
and transmits through the cosmic tide.

No wall can block, no space too far—
its wave extends to every star.

It speaks to past, present, and what's to come,
for all of time is played as one.

This now, dear Laddu, holds them all—
every rise and every fall.
Within this moment, still and deep,
the eternal frequencies wake from sleep.

A proper Pineal, clear and bright,
can pierce through shadow, time, and light.
It taps the past, the yet to be,
and present truths we fail to see.

All within the Great I's mind,
the conscious field of every kind—
where thought and memory freely blend,
and time folds in to meet its end.

But to receive, and to transmit true,
the body must be cleansed anew.
Prepared through breath, refined with care,
so sacred signals fill the air.

Yet even more, the mind must rest,
in calmness, joy, and blissful zest.

Only then the soul can hear,
and decode what all things whisper near.

A proper Pineal, clear and true,
becomes the guru that guides you through.
It speaks not loud, but soft within—
a whisper felt beneath the skin.

Each thought, each gut feeling, rising slow,
are messages from the soul's deep glow.
Even pain or pressure in the frame
may hint at what is soon to came.

The body speaks in subtle ways,
predicting tides and coming days.
But to decode these sacred signs,
to read the map between the lines—

One must remain in still delight,
in calmness soft and bliss so light.
For only in that sacred flesh,
do feelings bloom and patterns mesh.

The Pineal is more than a guide inside—
it's a transmitter, a manifestor's tide.
It grants our wishes, clear and true,
when aligned with the higher view.

The more we birth densityless light,
the faster dreams take holy flight.
Through Pineal fire, the soul does send
its will across where thoughts extend.

But calmness is the sacred key—
it tunes the wave, it sets us free.
For only in a peaceful frame
can frequency shed weight and name.

So cast away anger, ego's cry,
jealousy, and fears that lie.
All negative emotion must be released—
to let your manifestation feast.

COW—the Circle of Willis, divine and wise,
the power supply where the brain relies.
I see the brain as a sacred machine—
a processor where thoughts are seen.

The COW gives power, pulsing through,
fueling all the brain must do.
And at the peak, with vision wide,
the Pineal stands—antenna of the guide.

In Advanced Vasi, we begin to tread
the sacred path where thought is fed.

We don't just breathe—we refine the flame,
working with power and thought the same.

Through this breath, so silent and deep,
the Glymph awakens from its sleep.
It clears the waste, removes the stone,
unblocks the mind, and clears the throne.

By giving more blood to the brain's core,
the processor begins to soar.
And when it enlarges, part by part,
the "I" connects—the sacred heart.

The regions where the soul aligns
begin to stretch beyond their lines.
The working potential is then refined—
to a supernatural state of mind.

Receiving and processing grow so clear,
as frequency whispers draw ever near.
The body becomes a vessel of flame,
able to call the cosmic by name.

And from this state, without disguise,
we gain the power the seers prize—
to manipulate the cosmic force,
through mere flesh—the Siddhic course.

The frequencies, both sent and received,
through the Pineal, finely weaved—
are processed gently, just before
they touch the antenna's sacred door.

For Divine communication to be clear,
the processor must draw it near.

The better it works, the finer the tone—
the consciousness makes it fully known.
It understands and acts with grace,
on signals drawn from time and space.

But this depends on power's flame—
the Circle of Willis, source of name.
The more the power, the more we rise,
as unused brain parts energize.

And as they're used, they stretch and grow—
the mind expands, and truths we know.

9.Divine Light

The more perfect the Pineal grows,
the more the face of God it shows.
What was once hidden, dim, and far,
now gleams within like a living star.

When eyes are closed, we plunge to night,
but still, some see the sacred light.
While meditating, soft and deep,
a glow begins where thoughts once sleep.

Some say it's imagined, just a dream,
a trick of mind, a fleeting gleam.
But the practitioner, calm and still,
knows the light—they feel the thrill.

They've seen it burn before their eyes,
a eternal flame that never dies.
A vision not of dream or lore,
but truth the soul was made to store.

The photoreceptors deep inside,
in the Pineal, where visions hide,
are often blocked, their light suppressed,
by calcium deposits in their nest.

But with heat, and blood, and oxygen's flow,
the Pineal begins to softly glow.
Its activation starts to rise,
and light returns behind the eyes.

In the process of decalcify,
the veil lifts gently from the sky.
The light before sight begins to gleam—
no longer just a distant dream.

Yet the denser the sediment locked within,
the harder it is for truth to begin.
The divine light in this sacred flesh
requires the soul to cleanse, refresh.

During decalcification's sacred tide,
the photoreceptors open wide.
The crystals and the cells within
begin to stir, to dance, to spin.

Together, they create a show—
as light within the soul does grow.
And in the Vasi's breath-filled flight,
the darkness bursts into sacred sight.

Black, blue, and red begin to shine,
White, green, and yellow, so divine.

The rainbow hues swirl soft and bright—
a living aura of inner light.

Once the sediments fade away,
the divine light comes to stay.
No longer lost or far from reach,
it glows before physical sight, to teach.

A small tinkle, like a distant star,
a tiny spark from realms afar.
Then slowly grows—a rising flame,
till infinite suns bow to its name.

Yet though it shines with endless might,
it holds the coolness of moonlight.
This is the divine light, soft and deep,
that stirs the flesh from ancient sleep.

It speaks of enlightenment in every cell,
a sacred fire where truth does dwell.
The brighter it glows within our frame,
the more of our potential we reclaim.

For divine light is the soul's true meter—
the power within becomes much sweeter.
And as it grows, untouched by hour,
we gain supernatural power.

10. Cleansing struggles

When Mooladhara and Swadhishthana begin
their cleansing fire from deep within,
they stir the lust, long kept below—
a hidden dark and primal glow.

It rises fierce, like volcanic flame,
with heat too wild for soul to tame.
The intensity burns, the senses reel—
a hunger no illusion can conceal.

It swallows thought, it shakes the ground,
pulls the self where shadows drown.
The desire for intimacy floods the way,
like a roaring sea that will not sway.

The desire for lust becomes a flame—
uncontrollable, without a name.
It blinds the eye, corrupts the view,
makes all seem flesh to hunger through.

It makes us see with craving gaze,
each soul as fuel in passion's blaze.
It crawls across both near and far—
no line is spared, no sacred bar.

Closest, friends, and strangers too,
become illusions lust pursues.

It knows no bond, no love, no grace—
just hunger in a burning face.

These tests shall push us to the edge—
where souls may fall or make a pledge.
For those who give in shall be deceived—
and never rise, nor be received.

Those who pass the test with flame,
shall control the lust, not bear its name.
The desire, once wild, will bend and bow—
for they command its rhythm now.

They become the masters of the fire,
not slaves to fleeting fleshly desire.
Though tough, the path may burn the skin,
the true test lies deep within.

When the cleansing is truly done,
the fire of lust must be undone.
For if it's not held in control,
you'll waste the hormones that shape the soul.

These hormones, rare, refined, and bright,
are needed to reach enlightenment's light.

To let them spill in careless ways
delays the path and dims the blaze.

Yes, nightfall may occur—it's true,
a natural thing the body will do.
But masturbation must be stilled—
for it drains what must be willed.

During cleansing, hold the flame,
don't lose the gift for moment's gain.
If release is felt, then once in time,
two weeks apart is still divine.

For lust arises fierce and bright,
when hormones stir in cleansing light.
It is not sin, but sacred sign—
a storm to cross, a gate divine.

When one holds still through passion's flame,
they rise above all need and name.
The cleansing of Manipura begins,
with stomach storms and swirling spins.

Pain, gastric fire, and acid tide,
loose motion, vomit—none can hide.
The hunger swings from none to all,
a raging feast, then famine's call.

One moment starved, the next, repelled—
the body's balance strangely shelled.
This is the fire that churns within,
where craving and control begin.

The root of this chaotic dance—
is digestive cleansing's sacred chance.
Enzymes, fierce and pure, arise,
to burn the waste that spirit denies.

Through this, the core is purified—
and the flame of will is fortified.
Dear Laddu, the stomach trials we face,
will pass in time—so hold your grace.

The struggle may rise, fierce and wide,
but a divine gift waits on the other side.
Let not the pain bring you dismay,
for it's the body's sacred way.

In time, your form will slim and shine,
refined by nature's hidden design.
This is the will of life made pure,
a body cleansed, a heart secure.

And through this path, so clear and still,
you're filled with lymph of finest will.

Good quality flows where waste once lay—
and light returns to guide your way.

Anahatha—the heart so wide,
is the core where mucus dares to hide.
It holds the power, soft yet strong,
to nullify waste and right the wrong.

During cleansing, you may feel
a ball of pressure, firm and real—
stuck right at the chest's deep core,
as if the breath can't open more.

But Laddu, know—this is the sign
that cleansing is in perfect line.
So do not fear, nor push away—
just breathe, and let the body sway.

The mucus soon will rise and leave,
through vomiting, the body grieves.
But food won't come—just waste expelled,
the toxic veil from which you're healed.

Vishuddhi—the core of refinement true,
where cleansing winds come breaking through.
In this stage, you may cough out loud,
as mucus rises like a cloud.

It pours from mouth, both thick and fast—
a sign that cleansing now has passed.
But Laddu, do not fear the sound,
it's just the weight that's leaving ground.

In time, the storm will fade away,
and clarity will light your way.
You may feel an opening swell—
right at the throat's clear, central well.

When that space begins to shine,
know the process is divine.
The refinement flows, the truth is near—
your voice and soul will ring sincere.

The Pineal and Pituitary light the way,
and pain may come as if to say—
"We're here, awake, and rising strong,
you've walked this sacred path so long."

A spinning head, a sudden sting,
sharp pain like a vibrating string.
When this unfolds, pause the breath,
let silence guard you from the depth.

Do not fear or force the climb—
just rest, and wait for softer time.

When pain subsides and calm returns,
resume the flame that inward burns.

That dizziness, that folding spin,
is enlightenment blooming from within.
A sign, dear Laddu, you rise above—
touched by light, and shaped by love.

The heat refines the Pineal's core,
and sets the blood to gently pour.
With every pulse, it clears the way,
and helps the gland to work each day.

The breath, like wind through sacred halls,
awakens what in silence calls.
The more it sweeps this throne of light,
the more it shines before your sight.

Not imagined, not a dream—
but a rising, living beam.
The light begins to bloom and grow,
from soul to mind, a sacred glow.

Sahasrara, the Circle of Willis, divine—
the key to where reality aligns.
It scales the brain, in sacred flow,
through ACA, MCA, and PCA's glow.

The air and blood, when flowing clear,
refine the parts both far and near.
Each region enlarges, starts to gleam,
awakening thought beyond the dream.

The space within begins to grow,
and in that stillness, truth will show.
For the better the space, the clearer the tone—
the frequencies sing, and the self is known.

The single twinkling star before your eye,
whispers softly—now you can fly.
Supernatural begins to crawl in hand,
a sacred gift few understand.

But those who grasp without the guide,
may face karma's storm from every side.
For power, raw and pure as flame,
will test the soul that calls its name.

And if you do not know the way,
to hold the force and karma at bay—
then suffering may take its place,
and cloud the path with shadowed grace.

The common struggles on this way
will test your strength from day to day.

A cold, a fever, aches that rise—
back pain, nerve pain beneath the skies.

Gastric fire that churns within,
ear blocks, nose blocks, breathing thin.
Mood swings fierce, and cravings strong,
weariness that feels so wrong.

These are signs, not of defeat,
but that the fire beneath your feet
is working through the body's shell,
to break the walls where toxins dwell.

So, Laddu, learn before you rise—
how to move with truth, and see with wise.

11. Before the eye

This is not just a path of pain,
but also a path where miracles reign.
Yes, the trials are fierce and long,
but hidden in them is a sacred song.

The pain is deep, the fire is real,
so many turn before they heal.
They walk away, they close their eyes,
and never see the truth that lies.

For those who stay, who bear the flame,
will see the magic, without name.
It lives within, it shines so bright—
the soul's own miracle of light.

When the flame is lit, it starts to rise,
and colors rush before the eyes.
They swirl, they dance, they burn, they spin—
a storm of light that shines within.

It ends in fire, a blazing eye,
with a twinkling star just resting nigh.
Beneath it waits, in silent grace,
to rise and light the cosmic space.

It shines like suns, with boundless gleam,
yet cool as moonlight in a dream.

So fear not heat, nor blazing light—
for it glows with calm, not searing might.

The thoughts will whisper future sight,
in waking hours or dreams at night.

For those who listen, calm and true,
and decode what silence brings to view—
they shall succeed, and rise above,
carried by the Divine's great love.

No pain, no curse, no evil eye
can dim their light or make them cry.
Only the Divine grace will flow,
a rushing stream the wise will know.

It moves with power, soft yet vast—
a force no shadow's spell can cast.
Those who are wise will guard with care
the secrets whispered through the air.

For these truths are cloaked in flame,
and cursed to shield the sacred name.

The supernatural is not for show,
nor meant to boast, nor meant to glow.

It's not a spark for crowds to see,
but light to shape our destiny.
Its purpose lies in love and grace,
to heal our lives, to bless our space.

To guide the ones we hold most dear,
and walk the path beyond all fear.
Those who seek this for name and fame,
shall burn beneath karma's flame.

For if the sacred is used for pride,
they'll cycle through death and life wide-eyed.
Only the wise, the pure of heart,
may reveal this truth, and play their part.

Not for glory, nor to be praised,
but to lift the lost, to heal the dazed.
The unworthy who dare pretend,
will find their path has no true end.

They'll crawl in dust, stripped of light—
forgotten in the endless night.

12. Truth known

The truth has slept through endless ages,
buried deep beneath the sages—
that we are God in flesh and skin,
divine, both thick and thin.

But two great walls still block the way,
and keep our light from full display.
The first—impurity in form,
the second—disbelief as norm.

When the body's cleansed and heart believes,
the soul no longer grieves or leaves.
For then we rise, as we were made—
not born to bow, but to invade

the heavens with our rightful flame,
and walk the earth in God's own name.

The elites pollute both soil and seed,
with poisoned food and endless greed.
Through industrial smoke and silent lies,
they dim the stars within our skies.

They make us think our lives are small,
that we must buy to have it all.

Yet truth remains, so calm, so clear—
we have enough, right now, right here.

But the thought that someone else has more
unlocks a craving at our core.
We chase what's more than we require,
and feed the world's consuming fire.

While sufficiency sleeps deep inside,
we trade our peace for borrowed pride.
It's tough to find the secret books,
and even tougher to take a look.

And once you read, the path's still steep—
for understanding hides so deep.
Even when wisdom starts to bloom,
to practice it feels like a tomb.

Karma stirs and shakes the way,
disrupting light with clouds of grey.
To walk this path, both fierce and fine,
we need the grace of the Divine.

And kindness, dear, is Heaven's key—
for kindness wakes divinity.
If we are gentle, pure, and true,
then higher beings walk with you.

They'll hold your hand and guide your feet,
so you may walk in light complete.

13. The process

Now Laddu, come close, and hear me say—
the process of Vasi begins today.
The raw form I walked, with breath and flame,
is simple, yet bears the powerful name.

No golden cloak, no secret art,
just pure intention from the heart.
And what I teach is strong and free,
I call it the Three-Point Method, see—

A path so clear, yet deep as sky,
where breath and body unify.
Now take this gift, hold it near—
the truth of Vasi will soon appear.

Pinpoint the spot they call Adenoid,
the place where silent truth's employed.
This is the first, the sacred gate—
where breath begins to shift your fate.

Then follow forth, two phases rise—
the Sun and Moon beneath the skies.
To run the Sun phase, calm and slow,
find the Adenoid, let breath flow.

Then trace a line, with heart at rest,
to the lower stomach, near the chest.
Precision there is not the key—
just feel the flow, and let it be.

Then breathe, inhale, exhale, repeat—
and let the fire beneath you beat.
To run the Moon phase, soft and bright,
step gently into inner light.

Begin again with Adenoid's flame,
the first point, ever still, the same.
Then raise your gaze, both calm and real,
to the second point—the Pineal.

Let breath now flow between the two,
inhale, exhale, with focus true.
No force, no rush, just sacred pace—
a lunar rhythm, silent grace.

And in that breath, the mind shall clear,
as moonlight wisdom draws you near.
The Sun phase stirs the rising heat,
a flame that dances at your feet.

While Moon phase brings a cooling flow,
a gentle hush, a silver glow.

To balance fire and keep it right,
hold to the rhythm, day and night.

Let three parts Sun, and one part Moon,
be your measure, your sacred tune.
For heat must rise to cleanse and burn,
but coolness must in time return.

This 1:3 ratio holds the key—
to move in breath and harmony.
No mudras, no positions, no mantras to say—
just let the breath flow its natural way.

No need to bend, no need to strive,
just breathe and know that you're alive.
Never force the pace to slow or speed,
let the phase flow as you truly need.

In quiet trust, the body knows
how deep the sacred current goes.
And when the hissing starts to rise,
it's the sign—you've touched the skies.

It whispers that the tide has turned,
and through your breath, the soul has burned.
Use the Sun phase to purify,
to burn the waste, to cleanse, to cry.

Use the Moon phase calm and still,
to make the divine light bend to will.
Now the secret stands revealed—
no longer veiled, no longer sealed.

And Laddu, it's now in your hand
to choose the path, to rise, to stand.
Don't fret, don't fear the road ahead,
I walk beside you, soul and thread.

With every breath, I'll guard your flame—
walk with confidence, call my name.

Thank You

To Dear Higer souls, Deities, Angels
above, to Fate, Nature, and Karma's
tough love—

I bow with heart both full and wide,
for you have never left my side. Without
your grace, I would not be, I'd wander
lost, adrift at sea. But through your
hand, both firm and kind, you lit the
path and stilled my mind.

So once again, with soul laid bare, I
whisper thank you, deep in prayer. For
all you've done, for all you give, you've
taught me not just how to live… but
how to rise, to fall, to grow, and find the
truth I now must show.

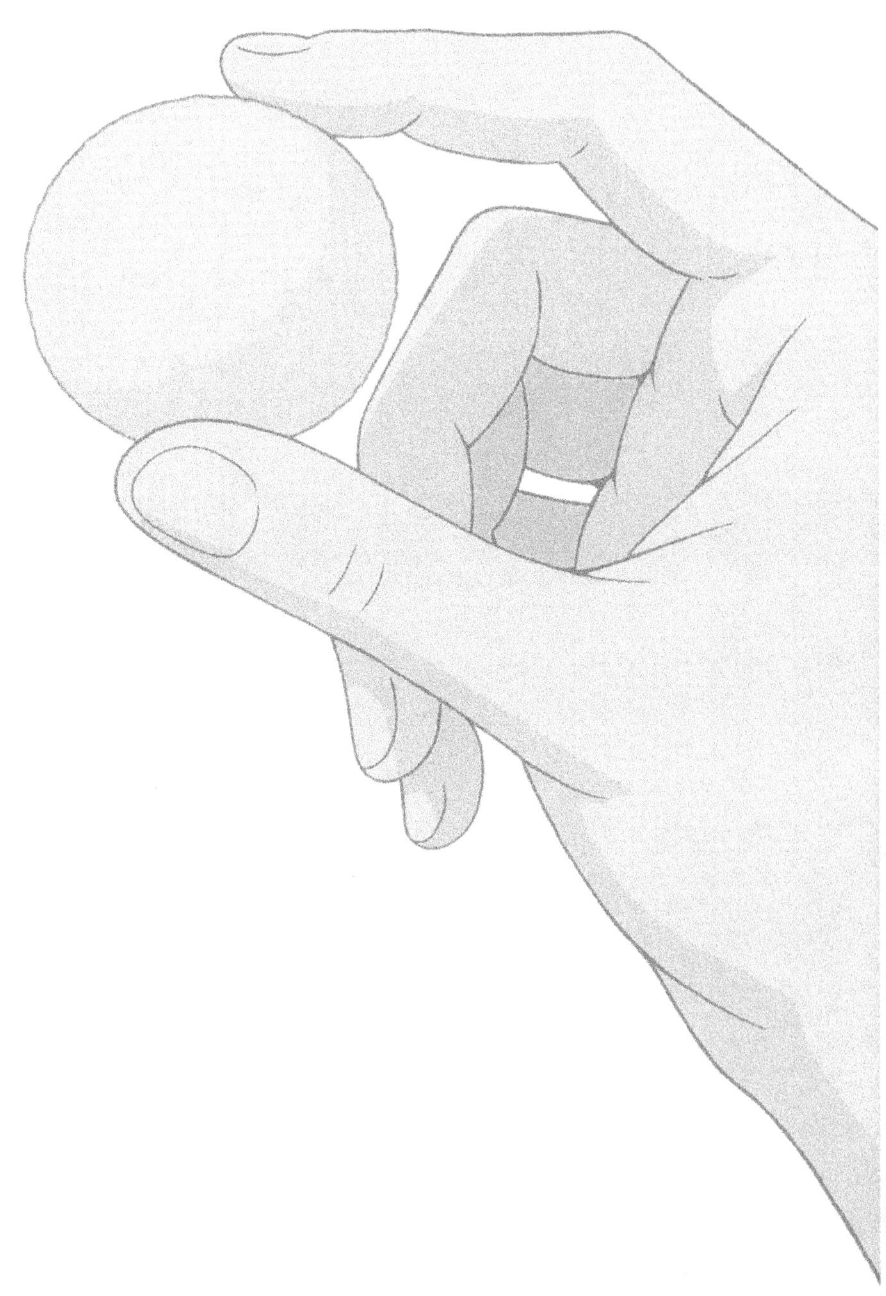

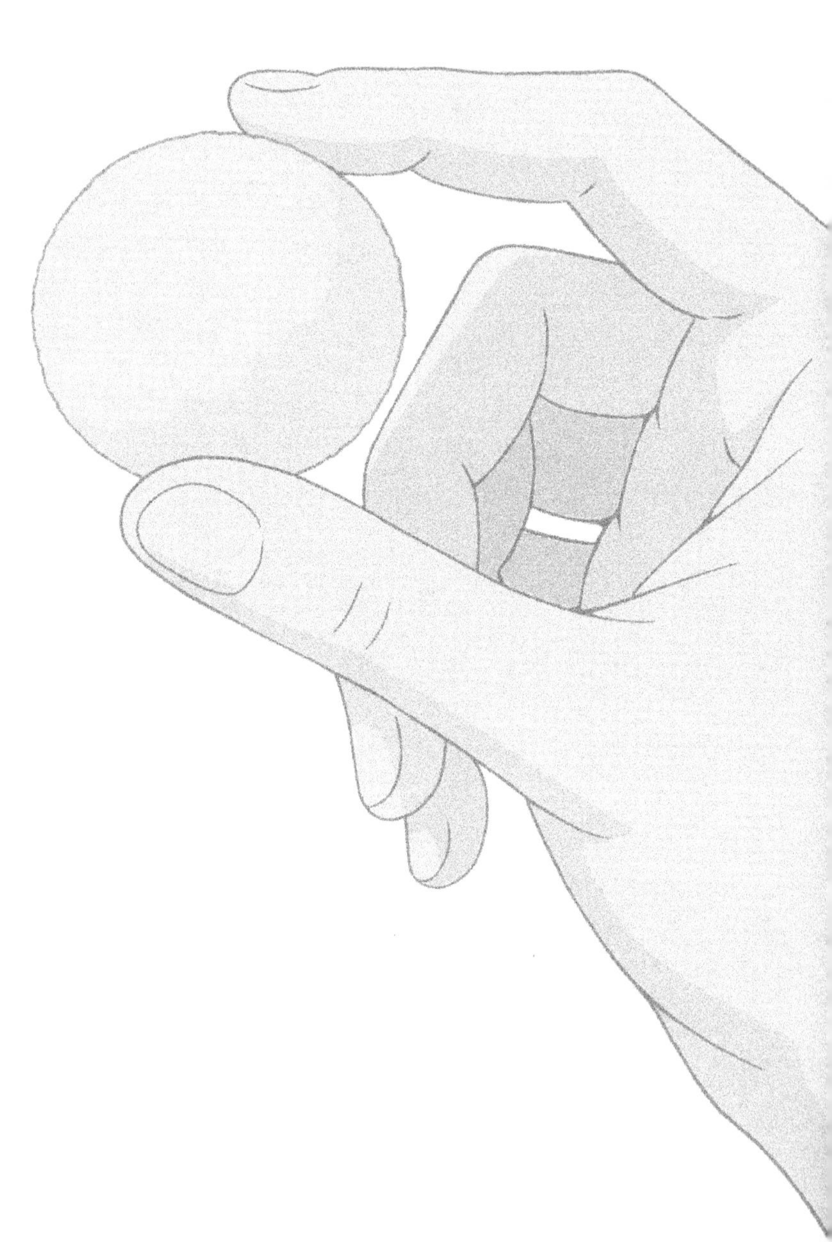

www.ingramcontent.com/pod-product-compliance
Lightning Source LLC
Chambersburg PA
CBHW040818120726
48005CB00012B/1452